THE POWER FOUR

PRACTICAL AND POWERFUL TIPS FOR PLANNING

ISBN 9-798895-049518

TABLE OF CONTENTS

In Loving Memory

Acknowledgments

IN LOVING MEMORY

My aunt, Rev. Dr. Joan S. Parrott. You always encouraged me to write from a young age. You would often say, "Steve, you're a natural writer, you need to write books". You believed in my potential more than I did. I wish you were still here to see it come to pass.

ACKNOWLEDGMENTS

Thank you to my amazing wife, Lonica. You have been by my side through all the ups and downs. You have always believed in me and continue to help me pursue purpose. I love you.

To my six children Zion, Jaylin, Mia, Alannah, Trey and ~~hannah~~Hannah. My world shines brighter with you all in it. Daddy loves you.

My Pastor, Ken Bulgrin. Thank you for being a spiritual father at a critical point in my life and ministry. Your guidance and wisdom ~~has~~have helped me grow tremendously as a man and minister of the gospel.

TABLE OF CONTENTS

FOREWORD

In this day and hour, creating intentional structure in one's life is more important than ever. It is a powerful strategy that we can use against reckless and aimless living. Unfortunately, this subject is often overlooked, and many people are currently living life like we tread water. They are putting in effort but are not making notable advancement toward their goals, dreams, and God-given purpose.

Frederick Parrott brings his experience and insight to this critical subject. In this book, he explains the transformative nature of The Power of Four: Prayer, Plan, Prepare, and Produce. Applying these principles through practical disciplines will not only make an impact on one's daily routine, but also develop a lifestyle of excellence. Ultimately, individuals will enrich every aspect of themselves in mind, body, and spirit.

This easy-to-follow guide will bring organization and calm to the chaos of each day. As an employer, I see staff members working stressfully to meet deadlines and bookwork timelines, and of course, deal with unexpected time-stealing distractions that appear out of nowhere. However, if every employee utilizes this valuable tool, it will increase motivation and a positive work structure. Consequently, employees will reach goals, produce higher quality results, and forward-think. As a pastor, I am confident that church leadership who use The Power of Four will encourage and inspire fundamental structural concepts.

In my personal life, I challenge myself each day with the mantra, *"Not One Day Wasted."* Time goes too fast to lose track of it or, dare I say, even waste it. Frederick states that, "each day we are given 86,400 seconds or 1,440 minutes that make up 24 hours." Are we using our days, hours, minutes, wisely, or are we wasting time?

In this book, Frederick challenges us to evaluate how we utilize our time. He starts the day with the priority and power of *prayer*. I agree that prayer is the top priority and the best way to start the day. It is the foundation on which the other three disciplines are built upon.

It is true that "you become what you do with your time." Choose wisely. You will find the time that you thought you lost when you apply The Power of Four!

Pastor Ken Bulgrin

INTRODUCTION

86,400

86,400. That is how many seconds there are in one day. Within that same day, there are 1,440 minutes that make up the 24 hours we each have to do with as we please. Why am I talking about numbers? You become what you do with your time. I believe that at the end of your life, you will look like the decisions you made with the time you had. I've come to realize over the years that people generally struggle with how to manage their time. Let me prove it to you. How often have you come to the completion of a busy and tiring day and said, "I wish I had more time", or "there is not enough time in the day"? I have no doubt that you are busy, have a lot of responsibilities and even are sacrificing time that could be spent elsewhere to read this manual. For that, I want to thank you for the investment you've made in yourself, and your own personal development. I value your time. Hence referencing the 86,400 seconds that are in a day. I've used about 60 seconds of your time so far if you're counting.

With that in mind, I wrote this manual because ~~everyday~~every day I talk to people just like you, who feel like they don't have enough time in their day to get things done. They feel tired, stressed out, overworked, overwhelmed, frazzled, often undisciplined, and ultimately unproductive. These individuals include every working class, entrepreneurs as well as corporate executives. What I realized over time is a pattern that became evident in these conversations. I noticed a common thread between the issues people were facing, and the reasons for them. Often, it would become apparent they didn't have an actionable plan, had no plan at all, had no particular goals in mind, lacked a clear direction for the day, couldn't account for how they used their time, and struggled to remain focused. As a result, frustration overcame ~~them~~them, and they eventually gave up. The common questions posed to me ~~daily became~~daily became "how do you wake up so early" and "how did you become so disciplined"? The answer may amuse you.

A little over ~~a year~~a year ago I got a promotion on my job that came with the option for more flexible working hours. I opted to work from 6 AM to 2:30 PM. I'm an early riser, generally up by 5 AM, so I figured I could have the rest of the day to relax after work. I forgot to tell you that my wife and I have 6 kids that range from age 5-16. I'll pause while you laugh at my ambitious goal of relaxing after a ~~work day~~workday, on a school night. You guessed it, after work the real job of parenting and marriage took center stage. I found that after getting the kids to bed and spending time with my wife, late night gym sessions did not give me much sleep before work the next day. I had too much energy after the workout and would end up ~~laying~~lying in bed wide awake. Before the promotion, I would workout at 5~~:00~~ AM because my job didn't start until 8 AM. That gave me adequate time for a great workout and to get cleaned up and ready for work. However, now with a job starting at 6 AM, I'd barely have time to work up a sweat before getting back in the car to head to work. Do you see the problem that was created? And before you think it, no, subtracting working out from my schedule was not an option. I needed a plan.

To fix this issue, I came up with the idea to wake up at 3 AM to ~~workout~~work out, so that I could be ready to start my workday at 6 AM. It made good practical sense, but my body didn't get the text message that we were starting a new habit. To motivate myself for the middle of the night or way before dawn workouts, I started making little videos to get me ready for the daunting task. They were no more than 20 seconds or so in length that I would post on my social media. I actually did it as a challenge to myself to wake up, get after it and go into the gym. The videos were simply me motivating ~~myself, and~~myself and holding myself accountable. What I didn't know is that I was beginning to motivate others by making these short videos. I couldn't tell in real time because there were rarely any people hitting the "like" button or making comments on the videos. To me, nobody noticed.

However, months later I began to get messages from people that I didn't even know, thanking me for a video I posted days, weeks or even months earlier. Others would say that I was the reason they lost weight, or that my videos helped them start working out again, or even to regain the motivation to live a healthier and happier life. Some people gave me credit for helping them become a more disciplined person. Several people even said some days they would not feel like working out until one of my videos showed up on their timeline, prompting them to get up and go workout.

~~Everyday~~Every day now people started asking me for tips on how to wake up early consistently, how to become committed to working out, and how to become more disciplined. I am still completely blown away by this. People in different time zones and countries were slowly beginning to look at my videos. People from places like New Jersey, California and Germany started to send me messages thanking me for how I helped them. No ~~high quality~~high-quality production, just me in a hoodie, holding my phone giving you 20 seconds or so of motivation and inspiration with a Bible verse or spiritual component with it. But the conversations I started to have with people offline about my videos sparked questions around the topics of discipline, motivation and planning. I began to see that often there was a correlation between lacking motivation due to a lack of discipline, which also impacted planning one's day.

I recall a time talking to a friend who was going through some difficulties, and in the middle of the conversation I just blurted ~~out, "~~out, "you have to pray, plan, prepare and produce". It was my way of giving a concise answer to a series of complications in his personal life. I ~~didn't know~~didn't know where it came from. I now know that was from God. I had not previously had this thought. ~~But,~~But this phrase completely summarized everything and encapsulated it into one sentence.

Later I started a podcast called "The Habit Hacks Show", and in one episode while discussing discipline I mentioned these four principles. After this episode a few people asked me to elaborate on what I said concerning the key points of Pray, Plan, Prepare and Produce. ~~So~~So, I did a follow up episode called "The 4 P's". Here I expounded on my ~~new found~~newfound system. I didn't know it was a system at the time of that recording. I was just happy to share something that worked for me. I had to find a system because of how hectic and chaotic my day was. Did I mention I was married with 6 kids? The beautiful thing about my personal discovery is that this system can work for you. What I have learned through creating The Power 4, is that a great system is critical to your success. You can plug your day into this ready-made construct and begin to experience the benefits of what prayer, proper planning and preparation can help you to produce. Let me follow that up by stating that while the plan is essential, you must also be flexible and open to making adjustments to that plan.

The worldwide pandemic of 2020 showed us that a plan often must be adjusted based on unforeseen circumstances. At this time, Covid-19 became a part of our everyday vocabulary. Suddenly you were forced to adapt to a new normal. It was not optional. It became common to order food from your phone and add the instructions "leave it at my door" for the delivery driver. "Contactless delivery" became the norm for many. Schools began doing virtual classes in the middle of the school year, forcing students and teachers to learn new software in real time. In like manner, many churches went virtual testing the capability and readiness of the local audio and visual teams. Signage that read "6 feet apart" would be marked all over floors of ~~market places~~marketplaces and businesses. The change was sudden and unpredicted.

That's how you must adapt to the changes in your life that make the previous version of your plan obsolete. You don't abandon the ~~plan,~~plan; you simply refine and sometimes redefine it. Acting as if change is not happening may be part of the reason you're frustrated. Many people I talk to daily kind of just let the day happen to them. They don't seem to be in control of it. Their day has no clear direction. The key is to always keep going and moving forward, but with a plan. As you go through this manual, I want you to ask yourself a few questions.

Does my plan make sense for me? Is this obtainable? Am I committed to becoming the best version of myself? How can I apply these principles to my life? Your success is largely determined by not just the quality of your plan, but your commitment to following through with the plan. That means taking action. The hardest step is taking the first one. The second hardest is to be consistent. So, are you ready to dive in? Let's go!!

PRAY

'More things are wrought by prayer than this world dreams of: Wherefore, let thy voice, rise like a fountain for me night and day. For what are men better than sheep or goats that nourish a blind life within the brain, If, knowing God, they lift not hands of prayer both for themselves and those who call them friend? For so the whole round earth is every way bound by gold chains about the feet of God'.
Alfred Tennyson

The first thing I will say about prayer is that prayer is not a waste of time, an item to check off a list or just something you do before brushing your teeth in the morning. In the same way, it is not something to just merely rush through before going to bed at night. Before you roll your eyes, believe me I've been guilty of this as well. I get it, wake up late, say the obligatory thirty second prayer and go about your day. There is an issue with this, however. Let me explain.

Have you ever been in a remote area and raised your phone in the air as if that would get you a better signal? Yea, you've done it. If your Wi-Fi connection or cell phone signal is bad wherever you are, then your connection and download speed is compromised and greatly reduced. It might even be cut off while you are in a certain area. There have been times when, due to my location, I was unable to make any outgoing calls. I was also not able to receive any incoming messages. It was extremely frustrating.

Prayer is your all access connection to the will of God for your life. It's supernatural ~~WiFi~~ Wi-Fi. Lack of prayer equals lack of connection. Prayer is communication. Philippians 4:6 ESV says "do not be anxious about anything, but in everything by prayer and supplication with thanksgiving let your requests be made known to God." You can't make any requests without communication, and you can't communicate without connection. Prayer is that connection.

May I submit to you that perhaps some of the anxiety, stress and fear we have in our day is due to a lack of prayer. If you are not grounded or rooted in prayer, you are likely subject to being overcome by any emotion or thought that captures your attention. It is then no wonder then that Philippians 4:7 ESV goes on to say, "And the peace of God, which surpasses all understanding, will guard your hearts and your minds in Christ Jesus." Did you catch that? Prayer leads to peace.

Reflection:
Consider what impact starting your day with
intentional prayer would have on your life.
- How can you begin to incorporate this
  principle?
- What positive changes do you anticipate
  receiving from doing this?

Habit Hack:
Prayer is essential. There is power in making prayer
the priority. Set aside time when you first wake up to
pray. This way there are no ~~distractions~~distractions,
and you have intentional, uninterrupted time in prayer.

Key Verse:
"O God, thou art My God; early will I seek thee".
Psalm 63:1a KJV

Notes

_____

_____

_____

_____

_____

_____

_____

_____

_____

_____

_____

PLAN

"Commit your work to the Lord, and your plans will be established."
Proverbs 16:3 ESV

Why do you need to have a plan? I answer that question with one word. Time. You can use and spend your time as you wish but one thing is for certain, you do not possess the ability to make more of it. Time is a commodity that once spent, it's impossible to get back. It is then critical to be very judicious with how and when you allocate the precious resource of time. What you ultimately become is a direct result of how you managed your time. And that is why you need a plan.

When I was a child, a teacher once ~~said~~said, "proper planning prevents poor performance". At the time, I only liked it because it rhymed and so I gave it no further consideration. However, at age 43 I see that my elementary school teacher was right, even if she was just remarking on how my late assignments were unacceptable. I was notorious for that. The truth is without a plan, you will likely fail or at the very least fall short of your goals. Proverbs 16:3 ESV says, "Commit your work to the Lord, and your plans will be established." ~~So~~So, the question becomes what is a plan and why is a plan important for me?

A general definition of the word plan is described as a detailed list for doing or accomplishing something. The key word here is detailed. Your plan gives you a very specific target to aim at. In addition, your plan needs a purpose which ~~also~~ should also give you clear and concise direction. These directional steps should be outlined in an organized way. This will help you prioritize and focus. Focus is critical because time management should be a key consideration in planning. Your plan should be structured in such a way that there is no wasted time, less stress and no procrastination. This plan should be so easy to read and understand that you could effectively communicate your message to anyone if you needed to.

Please understand, if you do not have a plan, you are opening the door to allowing something or someone else to dictate the terms of your day. Remember, you are in control. Though it may take time, sit down and think about your plan. It's your life. You are in control. Your plan is like a plant. It grows under the ground first which is your thought process. It develops a root system which you could call habits. You water the plan with the intentionality you put into it. Most people don't realize that even if you say you don't have a plan, you follow one or multiple plans daily. If you have a job, your employer has a plan for you to follow. Most jobs tell you when you can take lunch or breaks. You can't just show up or take days off when you feel like it without notifying someone. Why? Your job has a plan for vacation time, sick time and even a plan for people that take advantage of or abuse the plan that is in place. That plan is called unemployment.

We plan for vacations. Nobody just wakes up and ~~says~~says, "let's go on a family vacation to Florida today". No clothes packed, no hotel reservation, did not request off from work, nobody to watch the dog, no particular destination in Florida in mind, don't know how much money you have, you just go. That sounds crazy right? In like manner, it could seem peculiar at least why the majority of us do not plan for the day we are currently in. Often we do various activities that ultimately consist of our day. A good plan gives your day, week, month or year an identity and purpose. Without a plan, the words change and time will frustrate and derail you. If you aim at nothing, it is impossible to miss. It is also impossible to measure your progress. You need a plan. Did you know planning is also a biblical principle? Jeremiah 29:11 ~~NIV,~~ NIV says "For I know the plans I have for you," declares the Lord, plans to prosper you and not to harm you, plans to give you hope and a future." A good plan should give you hope.

Reflection:
"If you fail to plan, you are planning to fail". *Benjamin Franklin*

- How has lack of planning hindered your productivity in the past?
- What action steps can you take today to make strides towards effective planning?

Habit Hack:
Focus on your plan, not the problem. It's ok to make adjustments to the plan as needed. Sometimes a change to the original plan is not only necessary, but can save you time, energy and a big headache.

Key Verse:
"But don't begin until you count the cost. For who would begin construction of a building without first calculating the cost to see if there is enough money to finish it? Otherwise, you might complete only the foundation before running out of money, and then everyone would laugh at you."
Luke 14:28-29 NLT

Notes

_____

_____

_____

_____

_____

_____

_____

_____

_____

_____

_____

PREPARE

Have you ever rushed out of your house late for an event or appointment only to realize you didn't have the car keys, your phone or another important item, all while leaving the lights and TV on? It's ok, I have been guilty of this as well. You didn't lack a plan, you were just in a hurry, so you did not pay attention to the little details as closely as you normally would. This can be catastrophic or just embarrassing.

Details matter. While small, without the key, you can't operate your vehicle. Even though it fits in your pocket, without your phone, communication in the modern age becomes a bit more difficult. And when we are running late, we tend to get more frustrated as opposed to more calm. You see how things can get out of hand quickly?

Confusion and aggravation can arrive without invitation. Such is a good plan that is not properly prepared. Details are missed, timelines and key elements overlooked, unnecessary delays happenhappen, and your plan turns into a major headache rather than a huge triumph. You need a clear structure and strategy for your plan. How do you intend to successfully implement your plan? A plan without structure is merely nicely organized words. Your mindset becomes very important here and is key to preparation.

Get rid of all the clutter in your mind. Rushing is not your friend. A quote I love says "measure twice, cut once". In other words, spending a little more time in preparation is a good thing. Going over your game plan and rehearsing the critical elements is a good thing. Famed French Chemist and microbiologist Louis Pasteur said, "chance favors the prepared mind". How you prepare is likely how you will perform. And that preparation looks different for everyone.

Visualize your planned outcome, but also be mindful to anticipate potential changes or problem areas. Troubleshooting is a part of preparation. This will boost your confidence and help to give you positive momentum. Don't rush. Proverbs 24:27 NLT says "Do your planning and prepare your fields before building your house." Time in preparation now means less time fixing mistakes later. Don't think it tedious or laborious. Remember, measure twice, cut once. Preparation eliminates panic.

Reflection:
The way you prepare for something is an indication of how much you care about what you're doing. So, how much do you care about you?

- Do you give enough thought to preparation?
- What would being more prepared look like for you?

Habit Hack:
Time spent in preparation now eliminates time spent in panic later.

Key Verse:
"The plans of the diligent lead surely to abundance, but everyone who is hasty comes only to poverty."
Proverbs 21:5 ESV

Notes

PRODUCE

Now it's time to produce the desired outcome. To this point we've discussed the principles of prayer, planning and preparation. The three of them are excellent tools, but without production, they can't see their fullest potential. The plan you created is worthless without you applying focus, discipline, consistency and effort. You need to get moving and create momentum.

"Whatever your hand finds to do, do it with all your might, for in the realm of the dead, where you are going, there is neither working nor planning nor knowledge nor wisdom."
Ecclesiastes 9:10 NIV

This passage of scripture is a ~~not so subtle~~ not-so-subtle reminder that our days on earth are numbered, and that we have a very finite window of time in which to be productive.

Your production is largely impacted by your ability to focus and prioritize. It's one thing to write the words down, it's something entirely different to execute the plan. Start by setting clear and very achievable goals with the plan you've created. Be honest with yourself. The easiest way to start is to start. That was a bit anticlimactic I'm sure, but true nonetheless. However, the quickest way to stop is to try to do more than you can manage.

The advice I always give to people starting out on this journey is to make a list of things needing to be accomplished in a day. Now, prioritize that list with a top three. These three items must be completed before the day is over. If you can achieve more than three, I applaud you. Here is the key, do not get distracted, don't add items to the list without completing your top three. The goal here is quality of production, not starting things you don't complete.

Your production can slow down or stop completely when we add things like social media, tv or ~~non-essential~~non-essential tasks to your day. In moderation these things are great. I'm not saying don't watch tv and delete all your social media. I'm not a cruel person. However, at the expense of your plan, they are disastrous. The number one threat to your productivity is summed up in one word, distractions.

If you're unclear on if something is a distraction or not, ask yourself one question. Does this get me closer to accomplishing my plan? Some things are not necessarily bad to do, but they can derail your progress, focus and ultimately your goal.

Reflection:
- How will I apply the principle of production?
- What do I need to adjust in my life to become more productive?

Habit Hack: The best results come after purposeful prayer, planning and preparation.

Key Verse:
"No, dear brothers and sisters, I have not achieved it, but I focus on this one thing: Forgetting the past and looking forward to what lies ahead."
Philippians 3:13 NLT

Notes

APPLICATION

Success is a mindset. Regardless of what your "finish line" looks like, without an actionable plan, your goals are mere wishes just blowing in the wind. Now what? Where do I go from here? These are the questions you need to answer now.

You have just read four life changing principles that will take you from where you are currently, and transition you to where you want to be. This only happens if you apply the principles and concepts you've read. Application is key. Undoubtedly you have been through many stages. You've had an idea of what your plan looks like. It then became a written thought, and it is now ready to be made reality. Are you excited? You should be. You're getting ready to do something you perhaps previously have not been able to accomplish, and that is to take a thought or idea from start to finish.

Let me tell you, that is something worthy of applause. I know what it's like to be distracted, to procrastinate because you don't feel adequate or equipped, and to feel defeated as you fall short of your goals. But that's not you. Not this time. As a child I was diagnosed with (ADHD) Attention-deficit/hyperactivity disorder. It's considered to be a condition labeled as chronic, and meant I had difficulty paying attention in class, and was prone to hyperactivity and impulsiveness. The solution in the 80's (man I'm getting old) was medication prescribed by a Dr. I wish back then somebody would have told me about what I've shared with you concerning "The Power 4".

DISCLAIMER- Please note, I am not a doctor or medical professional. This is ~~not medical~~not medical advice. It is my experience with a real medical diagnosis.

The problem wasn't my hyperactive ways. I'm still an exciting, sometimes hyper husband and father. My wife and kids can testify to that. My issue was that I was not provided the proper structure for my learning style. I wasn't given a plan. Telling a creative person to sit still for an hour and look at the big green chalk board does not lend itself to a desired outcome. In that system, it wasn't created for me to thrive. That system was made for everyone to do that same thing.

But that isn't reality is it? We are not all the same. Your plan is not a one size fits all construct. ~~So~~So, let's talk about you. Up until today, what has been holding you back? Could it be that you didn't have the right strategy for success? Well congratulations, you have it now. This manual is something you can reflect on, read over and over again, and keep gaining insight. It is fully customizable for you to edit to suit your needs and goals. The principles are practical yet powerful. My prayer is that you conquer whatever you previously struggled with, and that you reach your

God given potential. Please be sure to pursue your purpose passionately. I only ask one thing of you. Share this manual with someone else. Well, you probably will have this one marked up with notes so, be a friend and buy them one. It's time for you to clock in. Let's go!

www.ingramcontent.com/pod-product-compliance
Lightning Source LLC
Chambersburg PA
CBHW031227090426
42740CB00007B/740